CW00499901

# TH LEADERSHIP SKILLS

*How to Use the Strengths of the Theory to Become a Charismatic and Authoritarian Leader*

by FRANK J. OLIVER

*Congratulation on purchase this book and thank You for doing so.*

**Please enjoy***!*

# Table of Contents

# INTRODUCTION

Envision an army of ants, multitudes of them carrying food and piling the food on a large rock. These ants are performing their task in uniformity and in a sequential order. The leadership is responsible for delivering the goods in order to maintain the survival of the ant colony.

On the human side, imagine a commanding officer of a unit assigned to a foreign country, responsible for his troops' safety, operating an efficient command post, defending his country, and operating as an assumed dignified commander.

"Success in leadership, success in business, and success in life has been, is now, and will continue to be a function of how well people work and play together (Kouzes & Posner, 2002)."

The two films which were selected represented a virtual-time situation, "A Bug's Life" and a real-time situation "A Few Good Men." Each film demonstrated a leadership style conducive to its environment and a communication style which revealed its strengths and weaknesses. Both films illustrated deception in leadership, the revelation of power in numbers, and the success and failure of leadership in action.

# Analyzing Leadership in the Ants

The main character of this movie was an ant name Flik. Flik was an army ant who had a creative imagination. His role brought challenges to the leadership team and forced them to make a decision to send him away to find an answer to their dilemma of confronting the grasshoppers. In the beginning of the movie, the ants are gathering food and marching the food up to a rock. This gathering of food serves a two-fold purpose:

First, to feed the swarm of rebellious grasshoppers, led by "Hopper" their leader, and Second, to secure the survival of the ant colony.

The story focuses on a colony of ants who seasonally gather food for themselves and a wild gang of rowdy grasshoppers. When bumbling worker-ant Flik (David Foley) destroys the food supply, the angry grasshoppers, led by the maniacally warped Hopper (Kevin Spacey) threaten to kill the ants if they don't produce a new supply of food by the time they return, an impossible feat. Flik leaves the anthill in search of help in the form of bigger bugs to wage war against the grasshoppers. What he doesn't know is he has actually discovered a group of down-on-their-luck traveling circus insects in need of a job. When the ants realize that their heroes are really circus performers (and the circus bugs realize that these grasshoppers are really big and mean) the situation goes from bad to worse. Ultimately the ants use their large numbers to overcome the grasshoppers. (Gore, 1998).

Yukl's definition of leadership basically defined the process in which leadership was demonstrated in "A Bug's Life."

Leadership is the process of influencing others to understand and agree about what needs to be done and how it can be done effectively, and the process of facilitating individual and collective efforts to accomplish the shared objectives.

Leadership was prevalent in all parts of the movie. The "Queen Ant" and the "Princess" were the female leaders who were born into their natural assignment by virtue of the fact they were the reproducers of the colony. They performed their assignment with the utmost of integrity, considering the safety and well-being of the colony. Because of this demand, their leadership skills reflected, "....consensus building, inclusiveness, and interpersonal relations, being willing to develop and nurture subordinates and to share power and information with the colony (Carr-Ruffino, 1993; Grant, 1988; Hegelsen, 1990;

Rosener, 1990) (Yukl)." The movie demonstrated how each ant was committed to the survival of the ant colony; thus, demonstrating the shared power from the leadership. Leadership's goal was to organize and protect the colony, laying down their life for one another if necessary.

A new command I give you: Love one another. As I have loved you, so you must love one another. By this all men will know that you are my disciples, if you love one another (John 13:34, NIV)

Although there was a Hierarchical type of leadership, the movie shifted the spotlight to the workers who were part of a "networking" which reflected the Paradigm Shift stated in Benus and Nanus book, written by Chronicler John Naisbitt (1997).

# Communication In The Colony

When Flik was sent away to seek help, he heard the colony cheer for his leaving. The colony was communicating a cheer of "yea, he is leaving" but Flik thought they were communicating a cheer of "yea, he is going to find help." Communication was the main element in this movie. There was:

Miscommunication - When the colony sent Flik away to seek help, they did not communicate the real reason of why he was being sent away.

Non-communication - When Flik hired the circus bugs, he did not communication to them the real purpose of their going to the colony.


**Body language was prevalent in the movie and reflected powerful emotions throughout the movie:** the face is the language of emotions. Different parts of it are used to display different emotions. Fear is usually looked for in the eyes, as is sadness. Happiness is seen in the cheeks and the mouth as well as in the eyes. Surprise is seen in the forehead, eyes and mouth (Latiolais-Hargrave, 1999).

Communication was a powerful tool within the colony expressing emotions, surprise, anger, and deception. The biggest turnaround in the movie took place when the Princess communicated to the colony to rally together and unify for the purpose of saving what generations of ants have fought for. Once the Princess realized the colony was more powerful in number and unity, they were able to defeat the grasshoppers and end their harassment. The model of communication which this movie followed was the Superior and Subordinate

Nonverbal Relationships: Appearance, Gesture and Movement, Face and Eye, Vocal Behavior, Space, Touch, Environment, Scent, and Time. This reflected the Higher Status definitions and the relationship to the Lower Status relationships (Goldhaber, 1993).

# Thoughts On Leadership

Today, modern corporate organizations face compound pressures driven by competition, talent finding and retention, globalization, financial expectations, technology innovation, energy trends, diverse workforces, environmental sustainability, corporate responsibility, the proliferation of the Internet, etc. The bottom line is that maintaining the status-quo or doing marginally better is not a formula for success. Change management and adaptation is ever more necessary to be able to set direction, to identify priorities, to manage complexity, and to deliver exceptional results.

John Kotter, Konosuke Matshushita Professor of Leadership at Harvard maintains that "Most US corporations are over managed and under led." In essence, today's managerial jobs require management and leadership skills with varying degrees of focus. The higher we go on the corporate ladder, the greater the demand for leadership ability. Thus, the increasingly fast changing environment we face requires more leadership from more people. To cope with these forces good mastery of leadership and management skills is essential in order to marshal and manage any organization effectively. Hence, the great need to institutionalize leadership development. "Institutionalizing a leadership centered culture-- where the business rewards people who successfully develop leaders--is the ultimate act of leadership." (Kotter 1999).

# Leadership Differs From Management

Webster's Third New International Dictionary defines leader as "a person who by force of example or qualities of leadership plays a directing role, wields commanding influence, or has a following in any sphere of activity." The strength of leadership comes from the enrolment of minds to a common cause or vision, and the release of intrinsic motivation to achieve extraordinary results. This means that anyone in an organization can be a leader, whether or not that individual is formally identified as such. Indeed, informal leaders are extremely important to the effectiveness of most organizations.

Allen Scherr and Michael Jensen offered in their recent Barbados Group Working Paper that "a leader is an ordinary human being with both a commitment to deliver a result--whose realization would be remarkable and visionary given the current circumstances--and the integrity to execute on this commitment to accomplish the desired results." One key idea of this definition is that "integrity" in the sense of leadership includes honoring your word--and that means either keeping your word or acknowledging that one will not be keeping it, and cleaning up any mess that causes for those who were counting on that word being kept." (Erhard et al. 36).

Kotter defines management as being about coping with complexity, planning and budgeting, organizing and staffing, controlling and problem solving. To this end, he asserted that management involves setting targets and goals, establishing detailed plans for reaching goals, allocating resources, establishing organizational structure, delegating authority and responsibility, monitoring results vs. plan, identifying deviations from plan, and planning and organizing solutions. Consequently, what great managers have in common is an appreciation of their strengths as well as an understanding of their limitations. Being aware that performance hinges on how well they figure out the pressures and priorities of their particular job, they find a course that works for them. According to Sternberg "finding this individual path to success is the hallmark of managerial intelligence.

Management is fundamentally about minimizing risk and maximizing adherence to plan and predictability. In comparison, leadership copes with the unknown, the dreams, and the vision that generates breakthrough performance. Accordingly, what one person views as possible may be a pipe dream to another? The subject of leadership is one where the results to be produced are accompanied by greater risk and uncertainty than what is normally considered to be acceptable in the realm of management. A scholarly gem of the Renaissance was Machiavelli's The Prince (1513/1962). Machiavelli's thesis is as good today as it was in 1513. It declared that "there is nothing more difficult to take in hand, more perilous to conduct, or more uncertain in its success, than to take the lead in the introduction of a new order of things."

Obviously, both leadership and management are vital for a well-functioning organization. It is critical to emphasize and understand Kotter's incisive conclusion about the tensions between leadership and management: ". . . even more fundamentally, leadership and management differ in terms of their primary function. The first can produce useful change; the second can create orderly results which keep something working efficiently. This does not mean that management is never associated with change; in tandem with effective leadership, it can help produce a more orderly change process. Nor does this mean that leadership is never associated with order; to the contrary, in tandem with effective management, an effective leadership process can help produce the changes necessary to bring a chaotic situation under control." (Kotter 7, 1990). This conflict can be useful; however, it is not a trivial exercise. Proper balance is essential for both short-term and long-term success of any business.

Leadership is about being comfortable with change, and understanding that the status quo works against progress in most cases. Every quarter and every month, there is change--things are in constant motion. While others may not be aware of this, leaders assume it. In knowing that change is inevitable, the true leader seeks positive change for a purpose and for the better. Kotter defines leadership as consisting of the following three elements:

1) establishing direction,
2) aligning people,
3) motivating and inspiring them.

This is a great definition but the paper of Allan Scherr and Michael Jensen, adds further insight into the domain of leadership by agreeing with Kotter's work but adding two more elements: "Communicating breakdowns, and managing breakdowns." (Scherr, Jensen 4).

Legendary leader, Jack Welch remarked in a WSJ editorial (2004) that after 30 years of leading he knows what leaders look like and act like. His process assesses four essential traits (each one starting with an E, a nice coincidence):

1) great positive Energy,
2) ability to energize others,
3) Edge or the courage to make tough yes-or-no decisions,
4) Execution follow through to get the job done.

He concluded his assessment with an observation about integrity and general intelligence as necessary attributes to complete the profile of a strong leader type.

As we gather, there is no shortage of leadership definitions. The many dimensions into which leadership has been cast can make the subject ambiguous. Nevertheless, there is adequate similarity among definitions to find common ground. Leadership has been conceived as the exercise of influence, as a function of personality, as a mode of persuasion, as particular behaviors, as a means to achieve future visions, as an approach to induce commitment, as a creative mind set, as an achievement instrument, and as a mixture of such conceptions.

# Situational Theories of Leadership

The inability of researchers to recognize conclusively all the dimensions of leadership resulted in the development of four popular situational theories of leadership. These theories propose that the most effective leadership style depends upon situational variables, especially the characteristics of the group and the nature of the task.

Hersey and Blanchard developed a "Situational Leadership" model that harmonized different combinations of task behavior and relationship behavior with the maturity of the followers. Depending on the readiness of the subordinates, the appropriate leadership style is first telling; then selling; then participating; and finally, for highly mature followers, delegating (Vecchio).

The most extensively researched situational leadership theory is Fred Fiedler's "Contingency Theory" of leadership. Fiedler used the LPC scale to measure the leader's orientation toward either the task or the person. The most appropriate leadership style was then determined by assessing three situational variables: whether the relationships between the leader and the members were good or poor, whether the task was structured or unstructured, and whether the power position of the leader was strong or weak. When these three situational variables created an extremely favorable or extremely unfavorable situation, the most effective leadership style was a task-oriented (low LPC) leader. However, a leader with a high concern for interpersonal relationships (high LPC) was more effective in situations where there were intermediate levels of favorableness (Ayman et al).

The "Path Goal" model is another situational leadership theory. This theory is derived from expectancy theory and suggests that effective leaders must clarify the goal paths and increase the goal attractiveness for followers. Four distinct leadership styles are proposed in the model: directive, supportive achievement-oriented and participative leadership styles. The most appropriate style depends upon two types of situational factors: the characteristics of the follower and the characteristics of the environment. Three of the most important follower characteristics include the locus of control, authoritarianism, and personal abilities. The three environmental factors include the nature of the task, the formal authority system within the organization, and the group norms and dynamics (House et al).

Vroom and Yetton's "Normative Decision-Making" model is also a situational leadership theory since it identifies the appropriate styles leaders should use in making decisions. The three leadership styles include autocratic decision making, consultative decision making, and group decision making. The decision titles determining which style is most appropriate include such questions as whether the leader has adequate information to make the decision alone, whether the subordinates will accept the goals of the organization, whether subordinates will accept the decision if they do not participate in making it, and whether the decision will produce a controversial solution (Vroom).

Although most of the literature on leadership emphasizes the influence of the leader on the group, the influence of the group upon the leader should not be overlooked. The relationship between the leader and the group implies a reciprocal influence. Groups have the capacity to influence the behavior of their leaders by responding selectively to specific leader behaviors. The influence of a leader can also be constrained by several external factors, such as organizational policies, group norms, and individual skills and abilities. Other variables have been found to neutralize or substitute for the influence of a leader, such as the skills and abilities of followers and the nature of the task itself.

# Managing Breakdowns For Breakthrough Performance

It is difficult to predict with certainty that the attainment of future visions will occur without the occurrence of some setbacks. Breakdowns are situations where the team realizes that the current plan won't work. Contrary to the general belief of people, breakdowns can be turned into the driving force behind breakthroughs. This concept is well captured with the saying: "necessity is the mother of invention". Breakdowns are opportunities for a truly committed team to find alternate solutions; this only happens by identifying the problem and working on it as a team. Expanding on the breakdown notion, there are two essential elements to every breakdown:

1) the commitment
2) the recognition and acknowledgment that, given the current course and speed, the commitment will not be realized.

First, if there is no commitment there will never be a breakdown; because in the absence of any commitment, whatever happens is acceptable. So, when there is no buy-in and commitment is unclear or vague, the existence of a breakdown will lack urgency, and may not even be visible to some or all of the people involved. Second, to the degree that one can accurately predict the outcome of the present course, breakdowns will be identified earlier, and thereby increase the likelihood that the issues will be resolved. On the other hand, to the extent we cannot see that the forecast of the present approach is failure, no breakdown will be noticed or, if it is, it will likely be too late to overcome the obstacles (Scherr, Allen).

The act of managing and communicating the existence of breakdowns helps to expedite the timely finding of new solutions and breakthroughs. If everyone is committed to the same overall vision, then a breakdown in another area that will prevent the overall vision from being realized is a breakdown for all. When a committed and motivated team faces a breakdown, they re-create their commitment instead of giving up. Renewing the commitment shifts people's point-of-view and often allows them to see opportunities and solutions that were not previously visible.

The quality movement offers methodologies (e.g., Lean Six Sigma, ISO 9001, TQM, CMMI, ACE, etc.) to help with the identification of some type of breakdowns by checking what is not broken and finding ways to drive continual improvement. Bringing in a fresh perspective to observe what is "business-as-usual" can help to spot breakdowns, which may have been invisible otherwise.

# Expectations + Commitment Is The Dialect Of Successful Leadership

Expectations and commitment play a central role in the effectiveness of leadership. It is known that leaders who expect more typically get more (e.g., Likert, 1961, 1967; McGregor 1960). By inviting each relevant individual to make a personal commitment to the realization of the vision, a leader is in practice working towards a self-fulfilling prophesy. The main implication of creating the Pygmalion effect by expecting committed players to excel is to drive high performance.

Eden (184) points out that "a leader who wants to be a more positive Pygmalion should point out to the subordinates that they have much untapped potential, and in general get them to believe that they can achieve more." Business schools teach many variation of this theme to develop leadership skills, i.e., Expectation and Self-efficacy Training, Immunizing against the Golem Effect, Avoiding Negative Stereotypes, Clearing the Record, Setting Challenging Goals and Objectives, etc.

Culture of an organization is closely involved in the realization of expectations and self-fulfilling prophecies. Schein has researched how culture impacts the effectiveness of an organization. In his own words, "productivity is a cultural phenomenon par excellence, both at the small-work-group level and at the level of the total organization." To this end, myth making is a promising way of molding organizational culture. Managing myths is a worthy cause for those influencing the culture "...the unique and essential function of leadership is the manipulation of culture." (Schein).

Think about the encouraging self-fulfilling prophecy aroused by the wide spread belief that "Nothing is impossible" or that "Will is the measure of power" compared to the Golem effect that comes from myths such as "Our products lack quality" or that "We operate on Murphy's law and the Peter

Principle". Therefore, symbolic expressions of a high achievement culture are important in the enhancement of expectations.

Business as usual is often the enemy of breakthrough performance and effective leadership. When things are very bad, the need for change is pushed in our faces. When a situation is unbearable, it seems that taking action is the right thing to do, and most are willing to work hard at it. However, when things are good, well hey, everything is fine. The problem with business as usual is that it leads to complacency and mediocrity, and over time such lack of leadership can be costly and detrimental to the organization. Napoleon offered his opinion about the importance of leadership in his famous quip that he would rather have an army of rabbits led by a lion than an army of lions led by a rabbit. Much like in professional sports the need for performance in today's competitive environment dictates the notion of "doing it now or it is not for long".

# WHAT DOES IT MEAN TO BE A LEADER

One of the biggest challenges of leadership occurs when you try to understand what it means to be a leader. Whether you're a manager, head of a movement or the CEO, you are bombarded with leadership principles that may or may not have merit. Those principles are categorized by time period, title, what's good, what's bad, gender, etc. I ask that you consider all of these categories are simply someone's conversation about leadership. They are not facts that are written in stone.

Yet, even though there is a wide range of conversations about what leadership is, there are still people who are uncomfortable serving as a leader. And there are others who don't do a good job as a leader.

Perhaps it is the fact that there is an overwhelmingly large network of conversations that pontificate "the right way" to lead. For example, some philosophies say the leader is supposed to be the smartest person in the organization. In others, they should be an intimidating person. They are believed to have the right answer when everyone is stuck. They should always be confident, tough, shrewd, etc. The list goes on ad nauseam. As a result, people spend more time trying to figure out whether or not they are getting it right, instead of providing effective leadership. If you consider this, you start to understand why so many people are challenged by the role of leader.

If you have studied leadership and the infinite permutations, there is a chance you are more confused with the limitless possibilities for which you should be and what you are supposed to do. While you have answers to the question of what leadership means, you still face many situations for which there are no solutions in sight.

Perhaps the very problem is the question: what does it mean to be a leader? As long as we ask the question, we will depend on someone else's conversation to give us the answer. There lies the problem.

Leadership is something you become. Asking what does it mean is analogous to asking what it means to be you. Whether you know who you are or not, you are still you. While no one can definitively tell you who you are, it is possible to know how you became who you are. If you understand how you arrived where you are, you can choose to stay the same or to become a different person.

If you look closely, you became whom you are as a result of a sequence of events that occurred throughout your life. You made choices as a result of those situations and shaped your personality and thought processes because of them. If for some reason you don't like who you have become, you can undo what you have become by choosing a new path. However, you will first have to know who you would like to be and what you would like to accomplish. Without that understanding, you are feeling your way through the dark and depending on luck.

The process of becoming the leader you want to be is analogous to becoming the 'you' that you want to be. For example, if you want a culture of 'yes men' in your organization, always being the smartest person in the room could help you get there. If you want a collaborative culture, you have to be collaborative and reward people for their collaborative efforts.

There were cases in my practice when these leadership strengths did not work. I remember a visit I made to a large company. A task force composed of the company's top executives had been given three months to generate a vision statement. I met with the members of this group and read the nearly completed statement. They asked me what I thought of their vision. I simply responded, "Who is willing to die for this vision?" No one spoke up. My question had surprised them and made them somewhat uncomfortable. They generated an isolated from their people document. I want to emphasize that vision must enlist and inspire others. And only in this case it can be considered as leadership strength.

It is easier to be an operational analyzer and taskmaster than it is to be a person of vision. Isolated and insulated people cannot succeed in motivating others. When they finally generate a vision document, its message will be frail and non-inspirational. Usually the "walk" of such people will not match their "talk," and the real message is clear. Nothing happens, and the vision document soon slides into decay and obsolescence. The challenge is to have real image of the future. Image that people cannot only see but feel, believe, commit to, and act on. Vision without reality destroys credibility.

A powerful vision does not emanate from the solitary musings of the supposed leader. Nor does it reflect only the "leader's" conception of the future. A vision that truly enlists and inspires others wells up from their deep needs and aspirations. Often, as we shall see, the way to achieve such a vision is by working with and through the people for whom it is intended. And the vision is credible because people can see that it is not a castle in the air, but a vision that is grounded in their lived experience.

Although there are so many individuals that assume some sort of position of leadership, very few actually becoming either meaningful or impactful leaders. The distinguishing characteristics often include the combination of one's attitude and actions taken, as well as how satisfied and what one is willing to accept, plus one's persistence and perseverance. When we attempt to understand what it means to be a LEADER, a mnemonic examination may be a great indicator and helper in terms of our understanding. Being a great leader requires: being an effective listener; evaluating what is needed, what is being done, and the best approaches; identifying alternatives; having a meaningful dream that drives one to a vital vision that creates motivating goals; proceeding with a high level of energy; and proceeding with actual resourcefulness.

1. Most people will say that they are good listeners, but while most people do hear, very few truly listen. When one makes the effort and takes the time to listen, he spends far less time speaking and much more listening to others. There is an adage that we were given two ears but only one mouth, so that we should listen at least twice as much as we speak,

but the greatest leaders dedicate even more time to listening, so that they are able to fully understand the needs of others in an empathetic manner.

2. Great leaders do not simply observe and intake information and data, but rather evaluate these factors in terms of how they can best be utilized and interpreted. The major difference between mere raw data and useful information is one's ability to evaluate, interpret, and put them to best use.

3. Do you understand all the possible alternatives, and proceed in an open - minded, non - prejudicial, unbiased manner? When some seeks the best way to proceed, he becomes a potentially great leader!

4. Ask someone who claims to be a leader what his dream.

5. You generally will not lead effectively if you are unable to communicate your message and motivate others to follow and take action. A great leader energizes those he comes into contact with, because his personal energy level becomes contagious in a positive and meaningful manner.

6. Nearly every aspect of life is a constantly evolving state. Therefore, only those leaders with the resourcefulness to adapt as needed, and the abilities and willingness to truly lead others, does what is needed to impact the situation for the better!

It is very important that you and I Lead by example. If we want others to do something they need to know we are doing it! Don't tell someone else to do something you aren't or won't do yourself. Be a Trend Setter! Follow your mentors and teach those who follow you to do the same (follow you as their mentor). Here is another quote from someplace, "Be a Doer of the Word, and Not a Hearer Only!" It is one thing to tell someone what to do and still another thing to do it. Here is a new word for you Exampler (Not Sampler). What Is A Leader? He is the person that Leads by Example (Doer). Now Let Us "Do Unto Others What We Would Have Them Do Unto Us!"

### LEADERSHIP TRANSITIONS

There is a growing recognition in the business world that a good leadership strategy can significantly improve business results. At the same time, good leaders seem to be rare things these days. According to recent study, it has been found that recruiting and retaining qualified leaders has become crucial challenge facing businesses today and in the future.

However, organizations are feeling the pressure of implementing a leadership strategy quickly and effectively. However, they seem to be faced with three interlinked difficulties such as:

1. They lack an understanding of which factors constitute an effective leadership strategy.

2. They remain unclear on the impact of leadership on organizational performance.

3. They are not doing enough to encourage leadership development internally.

Now first let us understand what we mean by Effective Leadership.

Effective Leadership is a self-sustaining organizational practice that transcends the personalities of individual leaders. The key to establishing a sound leadership approach is to identify which factors make up an effective leadership strategy and to understand how each of these factors affects overall results.

# Does Effective Leadership Influence Organizational Success?

Yes, Effective Leadership with its top seven factors does assign positive influence on organizational results. These top seven factors are:

1. Initiating and managing change: Organization must encourage a culture of change leadership internally in order to assert leadership externally. Today's turbulent organizational environment is characterized by a continuous race between competing businesses. Therefore, organizations must seize existing opportunities and create new ones in order to thr8ive. To reap the full benefits of change, they must also need to have a systematic change management approach that will enable them to react with agility and speed to changes within and outside the organization.

2. Communicating a Common Vision: In order to lead their organization successfully, leaders needs to have a clear vision (See Exhibit 1: Dynamic pattern of organizational structure) for the firms

and must also possess the ability to think strategically. Recent survey reports indicate, "Creating an environment of shared values and goals" has been one of the most important factors in improving employee productivity and financial results. Also a well-developed personal vision and the ability to sell that vision is the key skill needed for effective leadership in today's evolving economy. In order to create a culture of common goals, regular communication at all levels of the organization is required.

3. Empowering others to lead: Good leaders today understand that in the present economy, creating a culture of leadership and empowering others to make decisions are essential for long-term business success. The study shows that it is more important for an organization to have in place the systems and processes that enable leadership to emerge naturally and that is those systems that often explain why some organization outperform their competitors throughout the terms of many different CEO's and why some leaders can succeed in one organization and final in the next. The sharing of the leadership role is essential in the fragile and uncertain times that leaders face and will continue to face in the future. Teamwork and "Cooperative leadership" can only increase in

importance as a way of staying ahead of the competition. Leadership through teamwork also works to keep people, processes and ideas to check and to prevent a single personality from making foolish or irrational decisions.

4. Global Sensitivity: Effective leadership in the present economy must adopt a global perspective and must integrate global experience and cultural sensitivity. There is no escaping the trend towards globalization, which is presently taking place within organizations. However, organization needs to be ready to face competition locally and form global. In order to be well equipped to deal with the competition, they need to recognize the importance of having qualified leaders who are capable of applying a global perspective in their business dealings and are able to approach issues from different angles.

5. Cultivating Relationships: The ability to cultivate and manage relationships both within and outside the organization is an integral aspect of effective leadership. Forming and maintaining relationship with employees, customers and suppliers is essential to safe guard the interests of the organization. The ability to network effectively with relevant parties is essential because it maximizes

an organizations chance of capturing new business opportunities in the future and also enables leaders to learn from others and to gain expertise in new areas. Trying to walk alone in an increasingly competitive business environment is a self-defeating act, particularly since organizations are increasingly being rated on their innovation and knowledge capabilities.

6. Growing Top Talent: Building great leaders are a hot topic in today's business media. Due to a growing shortage of talent in the world economy, leadership skills needs to be developed internally so that employees can be prepared to assume leadership roles in the future. Retaining the people who had key leadership skills has found to be difficult.

7.Managing Performance: An effective leadership strategy needs to include a performance management system, which is geared towards positively reinforcing employees at all, levels of the organization and which is aligned with the end goals of the organization. A performance management system needs to involve recruitment and selection, training and development, coaching and feedback, performance appraisal and reviews.

Now let us focus on how leadership transitions bring about success in an organization.

Leadership transitions are a fact of our organizational lives. While times of transition can be exciting and energizing, they often prove difficult both for the leaders, who has new role and for the followers. Leaders work from the start to establish their credibility in their new position. In a sense, all eyes are on the new person, with some followers wishing for success and in many cases others pointing out the weaknesses that might prove to be failure.

During organizational changes, the needs of the new leaders and the followers often conflicts. The leader seeks to impact the organization immediately and the followers want a slow pace of change. Successful transitions require understanding both parties need and building communication and trust between them as quickly as possible.

During transitions four areas of interactions between leaders and followers are critical. These four areas are:

1. Partnering in decision-making: The new leader needs to understand the organization. Successful new leader's emphasis listening to followers, drawing out the issues that needs to be addressed

and the ideas that can potentially improve the organization. Followers can assist the leaders. Throughout this process by bringing to the table not only their own ideas but also facts and data that inform those opinions. Quality analysis of issues fosters significant conversations between the leader and the follower that result in effective decisions.

2. Successful Implementations: Followers play major roles in implementing organizational products and services. Successful leaders trust followers to implement decisions so that they can focus their own time and effort on defining successful outcomes. It is almost impossible for a leader new to the organization to know enough to be helpful in making implementation decisions. A new leader who does not shift to focus on the results the organization is trying to achieve deprives the organization of leadership and singles to followers that they are not trusted to understand defined outcomes and implement them successfully. The level of trust between leaders and followers is a key to success. Focused discussions between leaders and followers about successful outcomes and accountability mechanisms can results in focused and successful implementations.

3. Challenging the leader: The courage to challenge the leader is an important element in organizational success. Leaders benefit greatly from listening to employees and encouraging them to respectfully disagree. Honest interaction between leaders and followers can bring the leader new and important information. Ensuring that the top management includes those who have the courage to challenge the leader is particularly important.

4. Supporting the leader and the followers: It is important for the new leader to develop support networks of peers who can provide advice and counsel on the new role. In addition, the new leader needs followers to understand the basic functional needs of leadership. Given how over whelming the new role might be, just dealing with the daily stream of ideas, demands, e-mails and so on can challenge the new leader. Followers can assist new leaders by seeking information about their preferred styles of communication, not only how they would like to interact or the preferred means of communication but also what information needs to be shared with them.

Due to the current talent shortage in the economy, organization cannot rely solely on hiring leadership talent externally. Instead, they need to focus on finding ways to retain the best people and develop them into potential leaders for the future.

However, a leadership transition poses dangers and challenges for both leaders and followers. While each party naturally focuses on the organizations success, time needs to be spent on how the new relationship will develop and mature into effective working relationships.

# UNDERSTANDING THE FOUNDATIONS OF LEADERSHIP

There has been an attempt to understand leadership for many years. There has been and is being made a number of efforts to create a model or theory capturing key principles of leadership art. While detailing these efforts is not the purpose of this book, it is useful to look at some of the leading leadership concepts so that the reader can gain a better perspective on this important topic.

The tragic ending of Marilyn Monroe may have been different under her great and growing talent with a stronger foundation. Sustainable success requires a strong foundation in most endeavors.

Like a tree that can survive the harshest weather and time ravages successfully, successful leadership needs to be based on a solid foundation. And the deeper the roots, the greater the tree.

### *LEADERSHIP MODEL*

Leadership models enable us to comprehend the reasons why a leader acts the way that he or she does. One popular example of these leadership models is the Four Framework Approach. In this type of leadership model, it suggests that a leader can be placed into one of the four categories in the Four Framework Approach which include: Human Resource, Structural, Symbolic and Political. It also suggests that in some cases, one approach is suitable and there are also times when it is not. Depending upon a certain situation, a type of style can be effectual or not. One must be aware about the four approaches as relying on a single or two approaches would be insufficient. Aside from this, one must also be mindful of the limitations of supporting a single approach.

In today's fast-paced and turbulent environment, as a leader you struggle with the demands and burdens of assuming the mantle of leadership. You truly want to be a dedicated and effective leader, but you feel on the verge of burn-out as you face ongoing challenges which never seem to end. Your employees don't seem as motivated, they've lost their commitment to the larger vision, and they're not as productive as you'd like them to be. You're also tired of putting out fires and wish people would stop complaining, and just do their work.

And to make matters worse, you often feel isolated and believe that nobody really appreciates what you're going through. You ask yourself - who can I trust to share my burdens with? Where can I go for help to turn things around?

If you can relate to these issues, then I have a provocative question for you: Have you ever considered that your basic assumptions about leadership may be contributing to your struggles?

Let's examine some current leadership models and their limitations, and then propose a model that more effectively addresses the common problems confronting today's leader.

# Human Resource Leadership Model Framework

In the Human Resource framework, a human resource leader is easily reached and able to be seen, believes in people and communicates it. They also authorize, share information, support, and budget decision-making down into their association and boost participation. In the Human Resource Framework, the leader is a means and servant whose leadership approach is advocating, support and empowerment in an effectual leadership circumstances. In an ineffective leadership circumstances, a person's leadership style is deception and abdication and is an easy target.

# Structural Leadership Model Framework

In the Structural Framework, a structural leader focuses on strategy, implementation, adaptation, experimentation, environment and structure. In an ineffective leadership circumstances, the person's leadership style is details and is a petty oppressor while in an effective leadership condition, the person's leadership style is design and analysis and is a community architect.

# Symbolic Leadership Model Framework

In the Symbolic Framework, a symbolic leader uses symbols to get attention, find out and converse a vision and view associations as a stage to participate in specific functions and bestow impressions. They also endeavor to frame experience through providing reasonable understanding of experiences. In an effective leadership condition, the leadership style of an individual is inspiration. In an ineffective leadership condition, the leadership style of an individual is mirrors and smoke and is a fanatic.

# Political Leadership Model Framework

In the Political Framework, a political leader reviews the distribution of interests and power and makes what they want and what they can get clearly. They also utilize persuasion first, construct relationship to other stakeholders and employs negotiation and force if it is really necessary. In an effective leadership circumstances, the leadership style of a person is alliance and construction. In an ineffective leadership situation, the leadership style of a person is manipulation.

# Current Leadership Model

Our culture has no shortage of leadership theories and models. There is charismatic leadership, situational leadership, and transformational leadership to name only a few. Each theory has its own focus as to what makes for an effective leader, whether it is the sheer appeal of one's personality, the context in which leadership occurs, or the needs of the organization. In effect, they all attempt to answer the question: What leadership style must a leader adopt in order to maximize his or her effectiveness with followers? However, leadership style is really not the most fundamental issue to consider. Effective leadership has more to do with one's intentions or motives for leading. Put succinctly, the question is: Whose interests are you ultimately serving as a leader? How you answer this question determines not only your effectiveness as a leader but also the success of your organization.

A leadership model is simply a way of knowing and better understanding why leaders have to act the way that they do and make the decisions that we sometimes do not agree with. However, this does not necessarily mean that you only have to focus on the type of behavior discussed in the leadership models but these models is a means of understanding that each kind of situation identifies for a certain approach or behavior that a leader must take into consideration. If you want to know more about leadership models there are numerous resources online and in publication as well as some popular classroom educational resources that can help elevate your understanding and ability to utilize leadership models to benefit your classroom, team, company or organization.

## LEADERSHIP TRAIT THEORY

Leadership trait theory is the idea that people are born with certain character traits or qualities. Since certain traits are associated with proficient leadership, it assumes that if you could identify people with the correct traits, you will be able to identify leaders and people with leadership potential.

Most of the time the traits are considered to be naturally part of a person's personality from birth. From this standpoint, leadership trait theory tends to assume that people are born as leaders or not as leaders.

There is a lot of value in identifying the character traits associated with leadership. It is even more valuable to identify the character traits that followers look for in a leader. These traits would be the characteristics of an individual who is most likely to attract followers.

However, the idea that leadership traits are inborn and unchangeable appears to be incorrect. It is true that many of our dispositions and tendencies are influenced by our personalities and the way we are born. However, most people recognize that it is possible for someone to change their character traits for the worse. Someone who is known for being honest can learn to be deceitful. The whole idea of saying that someone was "corrupted" is based on the fact that people can learn bad character traits.

If people can learn bad character traits and become different than the way they are naturally through conditioning, it logically follows that they can learn good character traits as well. A person who is prone to being dishonest can learn to be honest. A person who avoids risks can learn to take risks. It may not be easy, but it can be done.

# The Theory

The trait theory is one of the oldest theories in existence seeking to describe great leadership. It developed off the great man theory which was popularized by the Scottish philosopher and teacher Thomas Carlyle in the 1840s.

Thomas Carlyle gave lectures on leadership in 1840 and cited highly influential figures of society with both divine and poetic abilities. These included Muhammad, Shakespeare, Napoleon, Cromwell and Odin (Norse Mythology).

These became very popular and brought to the fore the idea that great leadership was based on certain endowments the leaders had.

Having been influenced by Carlyle's work, Francis Galton wrote a book in 1869 called Hereditary Genius, in which he described leadership as an immutable property endowed to extraordinary individuals.

Apart from the qualities of leadership being immutable, Galton believed that they could also not be developed. They were simply inborn.

For a long time, this line of thinking was embraced until the late 1940s when some theorists began registering different perspectives of leadership.

Since the great man theory had shown the qualities of great leaders as what made them great, studies about the trait theory did not deviate from that. These studies centered on the traits exhibited by those leaders since these are what could be observed.

The research and studies spanned many years but the biggest contributions towards the development of this theory were made by a few notable researchers.

Below we look at some of the contributions in the order in which the findings were published. This theory enjoyed a lot of attention over the years, including being rejected at one point. It however got a new lease of life later and still exists in some circles.

<u>1948</u>

Ralph Melvin Stogdill makes public his conclusions of research and analyses. The analyses included work by other researchers spanning between 1907 and 1947.

In this duration, Stogdill compiled many findings from various studies, including one from Smith and Kruger (1933) which had concluded that leadership occurred among all people and not just "special people."

There were two major conclusions by Stogdill as seen in his findings.

#1. The number of times a trait was investigated was not directly related to its importance for leadership. He noted that some leadership traits had received more attention than others yet this did not prove that those with them were better than those with more of other traits.

For example, he found the trait Technical Skills in 18 different studies. He however found the trait Intellectual Skills in only 12 studies. From his studies, technical skills were not more important than intellectual skills.

The importance of this was to point to specific traits which were more important than others. In narrowing down the list of traits, it would have been easier to pinpoint potential leaders. Also, it would have been easier to identify those regarded as great leaders in history.

#2. The traits possessed by a leader must be relevant to the situation in which he is functioning. In essence, this meant that leaders in one situation may not necessarily be leaders in other situations.

Stogdill reached this conclusion by analyzing the group situations which had been used in many of the studies done. Whereas a certain group existed within certain situations, another existed in a different situation.

Looking at the leaders in both groups showed them to have different traits exhibited as required for the situations their groups were in. This conclusion is what brought about a new perspective to leadership research.

The general conclusion by Stogdill at this point was that traits alone could not be accurately used to define a leader. The success of the leader had to be studied on the basis of both the traits he had and the situation he was in.

This set the stage for widespread rejection of the trait theory as many scholars agreed that specific traits in a leader could only be useful in specific situations. As such, if someone had traits initially deemed to be leadership traits but the situation didn't require their use, then he could not become an effective leader.

After this rejection, some theories seemed to replace the trait theory. Some of them were the contingency model of leadership, managerial grid, situational leadership and transactional leadership. The traits which Stogdill concluded to be important for leadership were Intelligence, Alertness, Insight, Responsibility, Initiative, Persistence, Self-confidence and Sociability.

### 1959

Richard D. Mann, a professor at the University of Michigan conducted a study on many findings about leadership. Mann focused on the findings about personality and leadership in small groups.

Although he used more than 1,400 study results, Mann did not consider situational factors as of great importance in leadership. As such, his study suggested that indeed personality traits could be used to positively distinguish leaders from non-leaders.

Mann's conclusions have been said to be tentative. All the same, his work earns a place in the history of the trait theory since from his findings, he listed some traits which he saw as important for leadership.

These traits are Intelligence, Masculinity, Adjustment, Dominance, Extroversion and Conservatism.

1974

Studies on leadership did not stop and after his conclusions in 1948, Stogdill did more research. He analyzed 163 studies of leadership traits done between 1948 and 1970. He then compared the findings in this analysis with those he had in his initial analysis (1948).

The findings he published were more balanced in terms of acknowledging the need for leadership traits as well as the role played by the situation. Interestingly, the same man whose work caused the rejection of the trait theory was now presenting evidence supporting the importance of leadership traits.

Some of the key findings in comparison to his previous survey include:

Physical characteristics were not important for leadership. Initially, characteristics like height and weight had been mentioned as important for a leadership position. These were however proven to be complementary to a leader but not necessary. An example of how this was not crucial for leadership is by considering basketball players. Generally, good basketball players are tall. However, that does not automatically make them great leaders. In fact, their coaches are not necessarily as tall as the players.

High levels of energy contributed to the success of a leader. Highly successful leaders exhibited high levels of energy which helped the leader engage in physical activities. High energy levels also helped in the natural motivation of followers.

The age factor. Leadership was noted as something that starts early. Put differently, the potential to become a leader is evident from an early age. It had been assumed that only mature people could lead or have the ability to lead.

Stogdill's second survey showed that leaders showed signs of great achievement from an early age. And since what is evident in them is mainly their traits, this helped the theory further cement its place.

The traits that Stogdill's second survey concluded to be important for leadership are Achievement, Persistence, Insight, Initiative, Self-confidence, Responsibility, Cooperativeness, Tolerance, Influence and Sociability.

## 1986

Mann's (1959) findings were reassessed by Lord, DeVader, & Alliger (1986). They used meta-analysis to find out just how consistent the study results were. They intended to identify the traits which significantly impacted how people perceived leaders.

This happened at a time when male leadership was most prevalent in business and society. As such, it was quite natural that the traits picked would be reflective of the male gender. The traits identified by these researchers as important for leadership were Intelligence, Masculinity and Dominance.

<u>1991</u>

Kirkpatrick and Locke (1991) argued in favor of the uniqueness of leaders. They stated that leaders were very different from non-leaders and the difference was in the traits they exhibited.

In their conclusions, they cited a 20-year study by psychologists Ann Howard and Douglas Bray. This study found that from a sample of AT&T managers, the desire for advancement determined the attainment of success twenty years later. This was seen as drive towards success.

Whereas some individual managers showed less ambition than others, one of those rated as ambitious was ready to leave the company if his aspirations were thwarted. He would also make the same move if he found the challenge lacking.

They identified six traits as differentiating between leaders and other people. These are Drive, Motivation, Integrity, Confidence, Cognitive Ability and Task Knowledge.

<u>2004</u>

Towards the turn of the millennium, social intelligence made it to the list of traits to be studied. It was established that an effective leader is one who was socially intelligent. This is defined as the ability of a leader to understand his own feelings as well as those of others.

Part of what constituted social intelligence was social awareness, social acumen and self-monitoring. These had already been seen as being necessary for effective leadership and had been identified by several studies done on leadership traits.

Zaccaro, Kemp, and Bader (2004) concluded that the traits which were important for leadership could be said to be a combination of good levels of both IQ (Cognitive Intelligence) and EQ (Emotional Intelligence).

The traits they listed were Cognitive Abilities, Extroversion, Conscientiousness, Emotional Stability, Openness, Agreeableness, Motivation, Social Intelligence, Emotional Intelligence and Problem Solving skills.

<u>2006 and beyond</u>

The trait theory can be said to be undergoing more development since more studies on leadership traits are being carried out. These further studies seem to be fueled by the lack of a complete list of traits needed for leadership.

A major trait coming up in studies is charisma. Charisma makes you attractive. Others say it is charming, even bewitching. In itself, it is a powerful tool, at least going by how it enables those with it to gain massive loyalty and commitment from followers.

Jung and Sosik (2006) reported findings from a study intended to distinguish between charismatic and non-charismatic leaders. They found that highly charismatic leaders showed high levels of self-monitoring, self-actualization, motive to attain social power and self-enhancement.

One of the most popular leaders labeled as a charismatic leader was Barack Obama. He was very articulate and managed to deeply connect with many Americans.

In other studies, Hoffman, Woehr, Maldagen-Youngjohn, & Lyons (2011) found that charisma played a significant role in the success of a leader.

# Strengths Of The Theory

The trait theory of leadership has several strengths which make it worth mentioning every time there is a discussion on leadership theories. These are:

Supports the general idea that leaders are distinctive.

This theory does not try to show that anyone can become a leader. Since great leaders achieve goals others can only dream of, they often come across as a somewhat special kind of people.

There will always be a lot of marvel at the abilities which leaders exhibit and their followers always speak well of them. This confirms the generally-accepted premise that leadership is not for everyone.

Supporting this line of thought makes this theory stand well with many people.

It is supported by a lot of research.

This theory enjoyed a lot of research and gained widespread acceptance as a result of it.

This is usually the norm with any subject that receives a lot of attention. And in the case of this theory, the various people who devoted time to study it generally agreed on the basics. The only part of it where there were some variations was in the specific traits for leadership.

Provides a benchmark for identifying leaders

Providing specific traits was an obvious win for this trait. It made it possible to pinpoint potential leaders because they had certain traits.

At the same time, although the theory fronts the idea that leaders are born and not made, it was still possible to nurture the traits identified. Also, anyone who felt like they were meant to be leaders could use the traits identified as a sort of yardstick by which to gauge his potential.

### *LEADERSHIP BEHAVIOR THEORY*

Leadership behavioral theories take a slightly different approach from the theories of traits. The most important assumption underlying the theory of behavior is that it is possible to make the leaders. It tries to show that not all leaders are not born, but there are specific behaviors that can be learned to become leaders. So, that would mean being able to train people to become leaders. The behavioral theories also sound common sense in this regard, because if it weren't true, leadership programs wouldn't have churned out leaders. So, to start leading others, people can get leadership training. Simply emulating the more successful leaders, this is how many have become leaders.

Specific skills can be learned to lead. In this way, behavioral theories have provided a better perspective on leadership by demonstrating that leadership is not meant for specific people alone, but that anyone can be a leader since they can demonstrate leadership behavior properly. In a more positive light, it shows leadership and helps us take a more open-minded approach to leadership. The behavioral theories, however, focus on behavior and skills.

The theories of behavior have linked leadership to behavior. They show that leadership is based on behavior that can be clearly defined and learned rather than on specific traits. Behavioral theory also showed that there were two main types of behavior among leaders. The first type of leaders showed concern for people and the second focused primarily on production. Since these behaviors can be learned, it is not always necessary for people to be considered leaders with all the specific characteristics that were related to leadership.

These behaviors need to be learned, and for others people can learn them. Early research has also shown that both people and production may continue to be concerned about leaders. Their behavioral, however, was also to a limited extent successful. The other theories that followed, such as the Skills Theory, the Situation Theory, the Path

Target Theory, penetrated deeper into leadership theory and how people became successful leaders.

# There Are Two Important Behavioral Studies

Ohio State University (1940s)
As leadership studies that were aimed at identifying the appropriate traits didn't yield any conclusive results, a group of people from Ohio State University developed a list of 150 statements from their generated responses that included 1,800 hundred statements. The list was designed to measure nine different behavioral leadership dimensions. The resulting questionnaire is now well-known as the LBDQ or the Leaders Behavior Description Questionnaire.

As part of the study, the LBDQ was administered to various groups of individuals ranging from college students and their administrators, private companies including military personnel. One of the primary purposes of the study was to identify common leadership behaviors. After compiling and analyzing the results, the study led to the conclusion that there were two groups of behaviors that were strongly correlated. These were defined as Consideration (People Oriented behavioral Leaders) and Initiating Structure (Task Oriented Leaders).

Task Oriented Leaders

The task concerned leaders are focusing their behaviors on the organizational structure, the operating procedures (S.O.P.) and they like to keep control. Task-oriented leaders are still concern with their staff motivation; however it's not their main concern. They will favor behaviors that are in line with:

- Initiating
- Organizing
- Clarifying
- Information Gathering
- People Oriented Leaders


The people-oriented leaders focus their behaviors on ensuring that people's inner needs are met. Thus, by emphasizing the human relationship, they will try to motivate their staff. The task and the results are still focused on people-oriented leaders; they only achieve them by different means. Leaders with a focus on people will behave in line with behaviors:

- Encouraging
- Observing
- Listening
- Coaching and Mentoring

University of Michigan (1950s)
Lead by the famous organizational psychologist, Dr. Rensis Likert, the leadership studies at the University of Michigan identified three characteristics of effective leadership; two of which were previously observed in studies that had been conducted at Ohio State University. The study showed that task and relationship-oriented behaviors weren't of major significance within the world of organizational psychology. However it was the third observation that introduced a new concept, one of participative leadership!

## CONTINGENCY PERSPECTIVE OF LEADERSHIP

This is based on the idea that appropriate leadership style depends on the group members and setting (Mcshane S.& Travaglione T page 472) similarly effective leadership depends on a match between situation and leadership style. Contingency leadership theories assume that effective leaders must be both flexible and insightful. These contingency theories include

i. Path-Goal theory of leadership
This theory has its origin from the expectancy theory of motivation its states that effective leaders influence employee's performance and satisfaction by ensuring that employees who perform their best have a higher degree of need fulfillment than the employees who don't perform as much.

Path goal theory advocates for servant leadership where leaders serve followers by understanding their needs and facilitating their work performance. This is theory has withstood scientific critique better than the others (Mcshane S.& Travaglione T page 472). Path goal leadership styles are directive, supportive, participative, and achievement-oriented.

Directive – this type of leadership style provides the that the leader instills a sense of responsibility and has clearly drawn up what the manager expect of his subordinates and performance of subordinates is monitored and appreciated where necessary through rewards of for meeting specified goals or may be facing disciplinary actions for failing to meet certain criterion. Therefore the directive style is a task oriented sort of leadership. (Mcshane, S& Travaglione page 474).

Supportive- this Style is primarily to look out for employees' well-being. It is where a leader does not sit on the other end of the desk expecting employees to reporting to him but rather he works alongside the employees and getting to know them on personal basis and when employee are comfortable with their leader they perform better and the communication barrier is broken and there is a flow of information needed to efficiently operate (Mcshane, S& Travaglione page 473).

Participative- this Style of leadership encourages the subordinates to have a say in the decision making , the subordinates make suggestions that managers considers when making critical decision which is a good thing because there's a sense of belonging in the work place (Mcshane, S& Travaglione page 473).

Achievement-oriented- This style focuses on the competence of employees so the managers set goal and then evaluate employee performance (Mcshane, S& Travaglione page 473).

Contingencies of path goal theory

As a contingency theory the path goal suggest that each of the following leadership style will be effective in some situations.

Locus of control- people with an internal locus of control believe that they have control over their work environment, therefore this employees prefer achievement oriented and participative leadership. (Mcshane, S & Travaglione page 474).

Team dynamics –Performance –oriented team norms is the result of directive leadership which work hand in hand  with low team cohesiveness. Whereas, high cohesiveness is backed up is supportive  leadership as a substitute ,eg a leader may choose to use supportive leadership in times where an employees' performance is as a result of a loss of a loved one (Mcshane, S& Travaglione page 475).

Task Structure- the idea in this structure is to adopt means and ways that don't just end up being ideas but rather procedures that will make an effective system. In doing so participative leadership is directly related to employees that work under non-routine because the lack of rules and procedures gives them more discretion to achieve challenging goals. Supportive leadership should be adopted for employees in highly routine and simple jobs to help them to cope with the tedious nature of the work and lack of control over the pace of work (Mcshane, S& Travaglione page 474).

Skills and experience - This is a combination of directive and leadership. Directive helps directive leadership to help them know how to accomplish tasks and supportive leadership helps employees to cope with the uncertainties of unfamiliar work situations. Directive leadership is detrimental when employees are skilled and experienced because it introduces too much supervisory control (Mcshane, S& Travaglione page 474).

## ii. Fiedler's contingency model

This was the earliest contingency theory developed by Fred Fiedler and his associates. Biased on this model a leaders effectiveness depends on whether a person's leadership style is appropriately matched to his situation (Mcshane S.& Travaglione T page 476), this model suggested that the best way to lead depends on the influence and the degree of power a leader possess in a given circumstance. Below is a table summarizing findings of Fielder's Contingency theory of leadership?

It's not easy to identify effective and ineffective leaders. Fiedler suggests that's leader perform better in some situations but not all the time. Therefore effectiveness of a leader can be improved by changing the situation to match his or her leadership style. This can be by changing the contingencies.

Fiedler has gained considerable respect for his contribution on leadership knowledge. However his leadership theory has been gained numerous critics. This is because the theory only considers two leadership styles while other theories suggest that there are more complex and realistic array of behavior options. Evidence has shown that Training and experience are also factors that strongly affect leadership.

iii. <u>Situational leadership model</u>

This is the most common contingency theory among trainers. It was developed by Paul Hersey and Ken Blanchard, and states that effective leaders will vary their style with the readiness off the followers this model also identifies four leadership styles- delegating, selling, participating and selling. Leader member relations, task structure, and position power.

Leader member relations- this the extent to which a leader is supported and accepted by his group members

Task structure-This is the extent to which a leader knows what to do in a given situation.

Position power- This is the extent to which an organization gives a leader the means to punish and reward group members, and get the job done.

# WHAT'S YOUR LEADERSHIP STYLE?

It is important that as leaders, we are aware of our own leadership styles, and the effects of it. One of the largest mistakes a leader can make is to be uncertain about his own style of leadership, as when he can't make up his mind as to what kind of leader he wants to be, he'll not just create confusion for himself but for his team too.

Can you imagine if one fine day your boss wakes up and can't decide whether he wants to be a dictator or a participative leader? You'd never know whether it is fine to raise your thoughts or will you get a major lashing for doing so.

Often, friction occur not because the team disagrees with the leader's leadership style but because they are confused by their leader's seemingly random 'mood swings', where a matter is fine on some days but unacceptable on others. As such, it is absolutely critical that as leaders we have a well formed outcome as to our own styles of leaderships and what we hope to achieve by it, as well as its limitations.

A leader may also relate to his team and operations in a transactional or transformational manner. A transactional leader uses the carrot-and-stick approach in motivating his team- do well and you will be rewarded, err and suffer the consequences. He will run operations based on what is immediately most beneficial to the task, for instance, putting the best people for the work. A transformational leader, on the other hand, motivates by inspiring and persuading his team. He leads by example. In terms of operation, he will consider what is most beneficial to the team, for instance, putting the people who will best benefit from a task to fill the role.

## We have different types of leadership styles listed below:

- Authoritarian Leadership
- Democratic Leadership
- Power and Leadership
- The Charismatic Leader
- Transactional Leadership
- Transformational Leadership
- The Servant Leader
- Situational Leadership

It is critical to note that there is no one style and manner of leadership that should be considered better or worse, it is all a matter of appropriateness. The style of leadership we choose should very much be situation based. Considerations include the operations, the culture, the team members as well as our own habits. An autocratic leader may be more suitable for wartime, but a democratic leader may be more suitable for peacetime. It would be inadvisable to impose our will on a team used to having their own way. It would be wise to adopt a transformational rather than transactional style leadership on a team with a large potential for growth. It is also impertinent that the style we choose is one that we are comfortable with and can maintain in the long run.

Your leadership style depends on what you are trying to do. There are at least three possibilities:

1. You are in charge of a team and you want to know how best to make decisions.

2. You want to know how to motivate your subordinates to work harder or change direction.

3. You want to show leadership to people who don't report to you.

Let's consider each of these situations in turn:

The question of how best to make decisions is the classic leadership style situation. The original 3 leadership styles were: autocratic, participative and laissez-faire. The autocrat makes decisions and simply tells team members what to do. The word "autocratic" suggests being dictatorial, but clear direction can be provided without being heavy-handed. The idea is that leaders should be directive when time is of the essence, when subordinates don't know what to do, or they are not motivated. The participative leadership style is sometimes called democratic or consultative. The key point is that subordinates are involved in making the decision rather than simply being told what to do.

Consultative leaders gather input from subordinates but still make the decision themselves. Being participative or democratic means that executives and team members make decisions together. This style is useful when the executive recognizes that wider input will yield a better decision or when participation will enhance commitment to the decision. With the laissez faire style, executives let subordinates make their own decisions. This style is also called empowering or delegative. The conventional term "laissez-faire" has a lax implication, suggesting that employees are free to do whatever they want. But it is now more constructive to talk of empowerment so that there is no connotation of losing control.

You're in charge and you need to motivate your team to work harder or change direction. This is generally seen as a job for the inspiring leader, someone who can paint a vision of a bright future and the place in it of all who are required to help the organization get there. Ideally, you should be an orator along the lines of Martin Luther King or Winston Churchill. But how many leaders are this charismatic? Also, there is research that suggests dangerous downsides to being very charismatic. Such people can be too convinced of their own infallibility and can lead blindly devoted followers over a cliff. So-called transformational leadership is closely related to the charismatic type. In both cases the point is to inspire people with a cheerleader-like enthusiasm, creating the sort of awe in followers that is normally associated with rock stars. Realistically, very few people are like this and those that aren't can't transform their underlying personalities. However, you can move people with honest conviction and a well-argued case.

Suppose you want to show leadership upwards or to colleagues. Maybe you don't even have people reporting to you. In this case, the classic leadership styles do not apply at all because you are trying to show informal leadership where you have no authority to make decisions for people who don't report to you. To get people on side who can take it or leave it, you need to show how your proposal appeals to their self-interest, how your idea will help them achieve their goals. This is a delicate balancing act. On the one hand, you are trying to sell an idea that will be of great benefit to the organization but you need to enlist the support of skeptics, colleagues who may put their own interest ahead of the organizations. But if you go too far in catering to their needs, you may win them over, but your action is hard to classify as leadership. Buying votes is good salesmanship, but may not be considered leadership. We generally think that, when leadership is shown, people are persuaded to act for unselfish reasons, for the greater good.

Leadership takes many forms, but there are three styles of leadership that are the most prevalent. Good leaders do not take one form and stick to it - they look for the right situations for each style. However, good leaders do know what their dominant style is and capitalize on the benefits of that style. Let's look at the three leadership styles, and the potential pitfalls of each. Think about which style is yours - and how you can modify it in various situations.

## _AUTHORITARIAN LEADERSHIP_

Autocratic leadership is a style of leadership characterized by individual control over all decisions and little input from group members. Typically, autocratic leaders make choices based on their ideas and judgments and seldom accept followers ' advice. Autocratic leadership involves absolute, authoritarian group control.

The autocratic style, like other leadership styles, has some advantages as well as some weaknesses. While those who rely heavily on this approach are often seen as bossy or dictator-like, in certain situations this level of control can be beneficial and useful. When and where the authoritarian style is most useful can depend on factors such as the situation, the type of task the group is working on, and characteristics of the team members.

If you tend to use this kind of leadership with a group, it can be helpful to learn more about your style and the situations that make this style the most effective.

# Characteristics of Autocratic Leadership

Some of the primary characteristics of autocratic leadership include:

Little or no input from group members
Leaders make almost all of the decisions
Group leaders dictate all the work methods and processes
Group members are rarely trusted with decisions or important tasks
Work tends to be highly structured and very rigid
Creativity and out-of-the box thinking tend to be discouraged
Rules are important and tend to be clearly outlined and communicated

# Benefits

Can make decisions quickly, especially in stress-filled situations
Clear chain of command, oversight
Good where strong, directive leadership is needed

Drawbacks
Discourages group input
Can impair morale and lead to resentment
May impair or ignore creative solutions and expertise from subordinates

# Benefits Of Autocratic Leadership

The style of autocracy tends to sound very negative. If overused or applied to the wrong groups or situations, it can certainly be. In some instances, however, autocratic leadership can be beneficial, such as when decisions need to be made quickly without a large group of people being consulted. Some projects require strong leadership to quickly and efficiently accomplish things.

The autocratic style can lead to quick and effective decisions when the leader is the most knowledgeable person in the group.

The autocratic leadership style can be useful in the following instances:

It may be effective in small groups where there is a lack of leadership. Have you ever worked on a project with a group of students or co-workers that was derailed by poor organization, lack of leadership, and inability to set deadlines? If so, the chances are that the result will be your grade or job performance. In such situations, a strong leader using an autocratic style can take over the group, assign tasks to various members, and set solid deadlines for completing projects.

These types of group projects tend to work better when either one person is assigned a leader role or simply assumes the job on their own. The group is more likely to finish the project on time by setting clear roles, assigning tasks, and setting deadlines, with everyone making equal contributions.

It can also be used well in cases involving a lot of pressure. Group members may prefer an autocratic style in situations that are particularly stressful, such as during military conflicts. This allows group members to focus on specific tasks without having to worry about making complex decisions. This also enables group members to become highly qualified to perform certain duties, which ultimately benefits the entire group's success.

The autocratic style can also benefit from manufacturing and construction work. It is essential in these situations that each individual has a clearly assigned task, a deadline, and rules to follow.

# Downsides Of Autocratic Leadership

While autocratic leadership may sometimes be beneficial, there are also many instances where this style of leadership may be problematic.

People who abuse an autocratic style of leadership are often seen as bosses, controllers, and dictators.

This can sometimes lead to resentment among members of the group.

Group members may end up feeling they have no input or say how things are or what they are doing, and this can be particularly problematic if skilled and capable team members feel that their knowledge and contributions are being undermined.

Some common problems with autocratic leadership:

This style tends to discourage input from the group.

Since autocratic leaders make decisions without consulting the group, the group's people may dislike being unable to contribute ideas. Researchers have also found that autocratic leadership often results in a lack of creative problem-solving solutions that can ultimately hurt the performance group.

Autocratic leaders tend to overlook the knowledge and expertise that may be brought to the situation by group members. In such situations, failure to consult with other team members hurts the group's overall success.

Autocratic leadership can also impair the morale of the group in some cases. People tend to feel happier and perform better when they feel like they are making contributions to the future of the group. Since autocratic leaders typically do not allow input from team members, followers start to feel dissatisfied and stifled.

## How Can Autocratic Leaders Thrive?

In some settings, the autocratic style can be beneficial, but it also has its pitfalls and is not suitable for each setting and with each group. If this tends to be your dominant style of leadership, there are things you should consider every time you're in a leadership role.

Listen to the members of the team. You may not change your mind or put their advice into practice, but subordinates need to feel they can express their concerns.

Sometimes autocratic leaders can make team members feel ignored or even rejected, so listening to people with an open mind can help them feel like making a significant contribution to the mission of the group.

Establish clear rules. In order to expect team members to follow your rules, you need to first ensure that these guidelines are clearly established and that each person on your team is fully aware of them.

Provide the group with the knowledge and tools they need. Once your subordinates understand the rules, you need to be sure that they actually have the education and abilities to perform the tasks you set before them. If they need additional assistance, offer oversight and training to fill in this knowledge gap.

Be reliable. Inconsistent leaders can quickly lose the respect of their teams. Follow through and enforce the rules you have established.

Recognize success. Your team may quickly lose motivation if they are only criticized when they make mistakes but never rewarded for their successes.

While there are some potential pitfalls in autocratic leadership, leaders can learn to use elements of this style wisely. An autocratic style, for example, can be used effectively in situations where the leader is the group's most knowledgeable member or has access to information other group members don't. Rather than wasting valuable time consulting with less knowledgeable team members, the expert leader can make decisions quickly that are in the group's best interest.

When used for specific situations, autocratic leadership is often the most effective. Balancing this style with other approaches may often lead to better group performance, including democratic or transformative styles.


### *DEMOCRACTIC LEADERSHIP*

With notions of an empowered workforce, a democratic leadership style has gained popularity. But how do you get the best out of an approach like this? While it has a lot to commend as a leadership style, doing well is not necessarily an easy approach.

A style of democratic leadership is an open approach to leadership, where decision-making is shared and team or group views are valued and contribute to the vision, goals and decision being made. The Greek roots of the word "democracy" suggest that people are involved in power or control. Another way to describe this leadership style is to call it participatory leadership, capturing engagement and engagement ideas.

The Democratic leadership style (or participative) is a medley of both the authoritative (autocratic) and delegative (laissez-faire) and usually the most effective form of leadership. Participative (democratic) leaders are those who neither micromanage nor completely detach from their teams. Instead, they skillfully guide team members toward positive outcomes by helping them set their own goals and objectives, allowing them to take risks without fear of retribution and fostering healthy communication up and down the chain of command. The leader ultimately makes major decisions, but he or she seeks out and considers input from the team members. Let us look at a participative leader in action and see how he used this leadership style to his teams' advantage.

Trevys' first job at a five star luxury golf resort came when he was chosen to be a caddy for an older gentleman who played a round of golf every Saturday morning, weather permitting. Trevys was only 14 at the time, but he was as reliable as the sunrise - always on time and always did his best.

"You're a fine kid, Tr, a hard worker," the old man told him one morning as he handed him a $5 tip. "I bet you end up running this place someday."

The old golfer's words were prophetic. Trevys continued to work part-time at the club all through high school and college, serving as cashier in the pro shop, helping the groundskeepers, even bussing tables in the restaurant when they were shorthanded. He earned a degree in business and was hired fresh out of college to be the resort's general manager, but Trevys never forgot what it was like to be a caddy, a groundskeeper and a busboy, and he vowed to be the kind of leader he would have liked to work for all those years ago.

Although he had a comfy air-conditioned office, Trevys was rarely at his desk. He made a habit of visiting the different areas of the resort at various times so he could touch base with every staff member at least once daily. Some days it didn't quite work out that way, but he always gave it his best shot. Trevys' team members knew that if they had something they wanted to talk over with him, they wouldn't have long to wait before he'd be popping in to say hello. Face time with Trevys was plentiful, and his people loved it.

They also enjoyed the "town hall meetings" that Trevys organized every few weeks. He always made sure to schedule them so that everyone from the custodians to the president of operations had a chance to go to one during work hours, never during their precious time off. Most of the meetings were pleasant, low-key affairs at which the team would review goals and objectives and talk about things like how to run a more environmentally friendly facility or how to improve the stay of their clients. Trevys encouraged everyone to weigh in and discuss ideas freely. Whenever there was a major issue, such as budget shortfalls that threatened to affect people's jobs or a problem employee who was creating unnecessary drama, Trevys took immediate action.

Trevys was always completely honest with his team, knowing that such honesty builds trust, honor and respect - something he never took for granted. When he didn't know the answer to one of their questions, he admitted it. When he made a mistake, he owned it and did his best to make it right. When a team member messed up, he dealt with it swiftly, firmly and fairly instead of letting it fester and affect the whole team. When someone did a superior job, they were publicly and generously rewarded. When a tough decision had to be made, he asked for input from the team, but ultimately he took the responsibility and acted decisively. And he kept the lines of communication open at all times, even when he had to tell his people things they didn't want to hear, and vice versa. Trevys and his staff were all full and active participants in their team's success.

Trevys' participative leadership style was successful because it fit his personality and his situation. He was neither too detached nor overly controlling, and his people were well-trained, highly motivated, and able to function effectively as a group and rewarded for a job done well. Participative leadership requires outstanding communication skills, but like any other skill, it can be learned.

## Benefits of a democratic leadership style:

Invites discussion, opinions and views
Builds a consensus
Encourages the ideas and creativity of others
Recognizes that people other than the leader may well have ideas about a better way forward
Creates a shared vision and goals
Builds commitment as individuals agree together what needs to be done.

# Limitations of the style

Can caused difficulties when quick decision are needed in a crisis

Confusion if communication is not clear about what or whether anything has been decided

When people are in-experienced or don't feel confident they may struggle with being asked to participate

Some people may regard being asked as a sign that a leader isn't leading – "I'm not paid to do this – you are!"

# When To Use A Democratic Leadership Style

A democratic leadership style can be a powerful way to realize the potential within teams and organizations. That's especially the case because:

It fits well with the current ideas of empowerment and engagement of staff

It is particularly beneficial for helping get the best out of teams

If fosters creativity and ideas

it builds a sense of commitment and demonstrates that skills and expertise are valued

It makes time to think about important decisions that need everybody to be on-board

It is effective with knowledge workers where their expertise are greater than the leaders.

There are however some cautionary notes about adopting a democratic leadership style:

It can be demanding seeking to consult and achieve consensus

It should not be an excuse for procrastination, discuss, consult and then come to a decision and act. Avoid the situation of becoming bogged down in meetings that don't go anywhere.

# Think About Your Own View Of Democratic Leadership

What do you notice in others who adopt a democratic leadership style?

How could this leadership style help you improve your leadership approach?

How ready and willing are your team for a democratic leadership style?

## *THE CHARISMATIC LEADER*

The term charisma will be applied to a certain quality of an individual character by virtue of which he is set apart from common men and treated as gifted with supernatural, superhuman, or at least particularly outstanding powers or qualities. These are such as are not reachable to the common person, but are regarded as of divine origin or as exemplary, and on the foundation of them the person related is treated as a leader. Charismatic Leaders are often thought of as heroes that are capable to use their personal magic to lead others. But that charismatic charm can be both a blessing and a curse on community. That's because charisma can be used for the good of a firm or nation - but also for less-than respectable reasons.

Charismatic leaders lead with 'concern for people' and don't 'concern over production'. They are concerned with the needs of their subordinates and accept inputs from them. They are determined to create a comfortable, friendly organization and believe such environment will lead to efficient work and results.

Examples of such charismatic leaders are Adolph Hitler, Winston Churchill, Bill Clinton, Mother Teresa and Cult leaders. They all lead by reaching out to human emotion and grasping their trust, gaining their respect and loyalty, maybe even encouraging them to do whatever the leaders tell them to. Charismatic leaders are confident that such leadership methods will work.

They keep the vision of the company's future on-par with employee satisfaction towards their jobs. They are dedicated and willing to take on unconventional methods, sacrifice financial safety, raise risks, employee and personal time to reach their goal. They participate in actions that will create or impress subordinates.

Charismatic leaders are capable to use their individual charm to get things done. This can be a very influential way to lead others. Actually, such strong charismatic authority can be got over others that these leaders can make their supporters do some pretty exceptional things. Charismatic leaders have the capability to feel the gap that presences between what an organization is delivering to its supporters and what the supporters need from an organization. This permits the leader to create a vision of a future state that everybody thinks will be improved than today's environment. The charismatic leader often expresses this vision using descriptions and tales in ways that everyone can realize the vision. The supporters see the leader as one that keeps the capability to imagine the future with transparency. The supporters are also capable to see how they fit into this future state and consider it will be better than nowadays. Since supporters can see themselves in this future vision, they support the objectives of the organization and the leaders more willingly. Rather than resorting to compulsion, the charismatic leader creates confidence among the supporters.

# Advantages Of Charismatic Leadership

Increased Employee Loyalty – Because charismatic leaders are adept at motivating and inspiring employees, it is likely that leaders can encourage an increase employee loyalty and commitment. Their goal is to make employees feel that their work and talents matter. Therefore, it is likely that employee engagement will increase and turnover could decrease.

Leader Creation – Charismatic leaders and managers have an infectious personality that can spur up-and-coming employees to become leaders eventually. The qualities of these leaders can take on a trickle-down effect and become a part of an employee's eventual management style.

Higher Productivity – These leaders are exceptionally skilled at gaining the trust and respect of those who they manage. As a result, employees are more likely to adhere to the high expectations of charismatic leaders. The effects of this have a high probability of spurring increased productivity and better-quality work.

A Move Toward Innovation – Charismatic leaders are driven toward change and innovation that makes sense. Therefore, these individuals will always look for opportunities to better the organization and improve processes. This means the company can always stay up-to-date on the latest trends and organizational practices.

Establish a Learning Culture – Major qualities of charismatic leadership are humility, effective communication, and improvement. Because these leaders have focused more on growth then punishment, mistakes are treated as learning opportunities. Employees are encouraged to find another solution to problems when the original plan did not work. This could create a setting where employees feel more comfortable taking a risk and finding better solutions.

# Disadvantages Of Charismatic Leadership

Wrong Focus – The main difference between charismatic and transformational leadership is the focus on ethics. Charismatic leadership can become more so about the personality and belief system of the individual. Their power to influence others could drive them to become arrogant and shun humility or compassion.

The Creation of "yes-men" – Because the personality of these leaders can turn admirers into followers, it is easy for their big personalities to create "yes-men." As a result, the ideas of a charismatic leader could go unchallenged leading to the implementation of plans that are less than favorable.

The Company Suffers if They Leave – To no fault of their own, a good and effective charismatic leader may have been the backbone of the business. Their tenacity, drive, and leadership could have caused many to depend on their ability without developing their own. As a result, their departure could leave a hole that no one has been trained to fill.

A Lack of Clarity – If a leader has delivered more successes than failures then they can start to rest on their charismatic abilities and forget to employ tactics that are also responsible for success: consulting the team, looking at previous performance data, and remembering the mission and vision of the company.

## *TRANSACTIONAL LEADERSHIPS*

A transactional leader is someone who, as the name imply, relates to his team and tasks in terms of "transactions". His decisions are often based on tangible benefits and losses, rewards and punishments, results and performances. Between a transactional and transformational leader, the transactional leader is a much more common species.

Transactional leadership involves a relationship between the leader or manager and his team that is carrot-and-stick in nature. This means to say that team members are rewarded when they carry out an action that benefits the team's performance, and they are punished when they take an action which is detrimental to the team's performance. Rewards and punishment are often used to signal to the team as to the appropriate and desirable action to take. Evidently, the transactional leadership style is very much based on "exchanges" in favors and debts, or "transactions". As such, it is also worthy to note that a transactional leader is often also an autocratic leader as he enlists the use of punishment and reward to motivate his team.

In terms of operations, a transactional leader may be considered to be task oriented. A transactional leader makes decisions based on what produces best results. That is to say, a transactional leader would allocate resources, manpower, time and money based on what he believes would suit the immediate outcome the most, for instance, putting the best people for the job.

As seen, the transactional leader is very much outcome oriented. This leadership trait renders the transactional leadership model useful to get results. It would be especially effective when short term success in needed while long term performance is secondary.

However, should long term performance be equally important, the transactional leadership style would be less desirable as it has little emphasis on investment of resources, such as people development and asset growth.

Transactional leadership is a reward and punishment style which is good at encouraging employees into becoming constructive and resourceful team members. The reward that is available if the employee becomes productive is a great incentive. Additionally, this style of management allows employees to realize that management is watching how they work and that they are intent on reaching certain goals and expecting maximum performance. Failure to maintain proper performance could result in punishment. This style also provides for short-term planning helping to ensure that the company's vision is met.

Transactional leadership is also comprised of a makeup that is clear and succinct. Employees of a company with this kind of style of leadership are conversant in what the company expects from them. They are also provided with obvious instructions and are required to follow a chain of command which makes it simpler for them to know which channel to follow. This also makes them aware that they will be rewarded for following directives and completing their tasks and punished if they do not.

Transactional leadership is useful in helping to increase production and to reduce costs. Transactional leadership is a style that has a clear structure with unchangeable policies and rules.

Even though employees have a certain amount of freedom and independence for performing their jobs, they do have to work within the parameters set out by management. Complaints or insubordination is not tolerated due to the inflexibility of the expectations. These leaders generally find it hard to adjust to certain situations and they do limit creativity.

This leadership style prevents managers from accepting creativity from employees who might have a better way to perform a job and does not accept suggestions for the betterment of the company. Since this leadership style is rigid and not conducive to suggestions from people under the management, this hinder creativity from employees who might have high-quality and effective suggestions for the improvement of the organization

Transactional leaders must operate within the boundaries set out for them and managers cannot react to emotions of employees so long as tasks are completed properly. These leaders can be effective at achieving goals within a specific time-frame but are unable to allow for emotional ties to employees. Employees then become insensitive to showing concern for the company and merely become performers to tasks. Although this leadership style is still prevalent, one will rarely if ever see a level 4 or 5 leader practicing this style.

## _TRANSFOMATIONAL LEADERSHIP_

A transformational leader is the opposite of a transactional leader. A transformational leader is one who motivates his team by inspiring loyalty and confidence in them. He takes the operations of the team to greater heights by working on the units that run the operations- people.

A transformational leader works his team through inspiration and persuasion. Rather than using the carrot-and-stick method of motivation, the transformational leader chooses to persuade his team to follow him via inspiring the team to gain confidence in him and themselves, allowing them to willingly commit to his cause and stand by him. This is often seen in charismatic war heroes in the movies such as Alexander the Great or Aaragon from the Lord of the Rings who yell an empowering war cry after a heartwarming speech and lead their men into battle. Besides requiring charisma and persuasion skills, transformational leadership also often requires the leader or manager to lead by example. It is through their action that they touch the hearts of their followers, and it is the strength of this faith that they create that makes their follower hold firm and loyal in the face of adversity. What does he believe in?

A transformational leader believes that passion and vision are prerequisites for a leader trying to inspire others. Not only that, a leader can get his followers to buy into his vision, only if he generates sufficient enthusiasm in them by displaying the same energy and enthusiasm himself.

How does he translate his beliefs into action?

The first and most important component of transformational leadership is a clearly defined vision, which the leader or senior management team is totally committed to. Mouthing mere platitudes will not work, and will fool no one. Belief has to start right at the top for it to go all the way down.

Then there's the all-important process of actually securing buy-in from all the participants. That's easier said than done. Since transformational leadership by definition seeks to change, it's never easy to implement. Some leaders might have radical views which will not go down well, especially if there's an "old guard" in place. The only way to succeed is to persist till the idea is finally sold. Again, it rarely ends with a single idea, so transformational leadership is essentially a continuous process.

A transformational leader is far sighted in terms of operations. Rather than being too caught up in the day-to-day affairs, the transformational leader looks beyond to concern himself with larger issues such as team dynamics, visioning, goals setting and people development.

People development in particular. A transformational leader is always concerned with developing his team. He looks at tasks as opportunities to develop his team members rather than as jobs for them to complete. He sees the development and growth of each and every team member as his obligation and will go out of his way to ensure that they are always in the process of growth and learning.

This also makes transformational leadership process oriented. As a transformational leader is more focused on development rather than results, he would place a much larger emphasis on a value-added process rather than a good outcome. This mean to say, a transformational leader would rather put a weak member for the job, knowing that it would be a beneficial experience for him but may be detrimental to the results, and not put a top player for the job, knowing that it'll produce the best results but not really benefit him.

Many famous politicians are transformational leaders. Via the skill of persuasion, they have United Nations and inspired faith. Examples include Winston Churchill and 'V for victory', President Obama and 'Hope we can belief in'. War leaders may also have to be transformational in nature as it requires strong commitment and loyalty to be inspired in soldiers to have them pick up their arms to fight even in the face of death.

Where's the catch?

Yes, of course there are some. Since transformational leadership feeds on change, it may not work in a situation where things are pretty much in order. After all, if it aren't broke, don't fix it - and this can be quite frustrating from the leader's point of view. Also, not everyone can sustain the high energy levels expected, and may give up or worse, opt out. And most important, just because the leader believes passionately in something doesn't necessarily mean that it is right for the organization. While transformational leadership can help create a trailblazing path, it could also plunge a business headlong into disaster.


### SERVANT LEADER

Servant leadership has been around for quite a while now. Not everyone has heard of it but the concept has an increasing number of devoted fans.

Servant leaders put the needs of followers ahead of their own. Instead of being domineering and self-serving, they put the needs of employees first. The idea is that doing so will motivate them to perform at a higher level and help them achieve their full potential, both for their own benefit and that of the organization.

In an essay by Robert K. Greenleaf, the author coins the term "servant leader." Exactly what is a servant leader? Are there any in your organization? If you don't have any servant leaders, how can you develop them? The answers to these questions may surprise you and introduce you to a vital source of leadership for your business.

A servant leader is one who draws their authority not from their superiors or by their position, but from their followers. A servant leader is perhaps the most fundamental and valuable source of leadership you will find within your organization. To draw power from followers gives the leader a measure of trust and respect that cannot be gained simply by virtue of title or position. The concept here is simple: the group members collectively give a fellow member of the team the role of leader. The foundation of this transition is trust and respect. These are leaders that the group will follow anywhere and forgo limits and constraints on the degree of authority granted.

A servant leader is first a servant. They are someone who has spent time in the line and learned in minute detail the functions of the group.

They have served as a loyal team member and contributed more than their share to the overall success of the group. It is important to look at the term "servant" without prejudice. Servant does not mean doormat or saint. A servant is not a selfless, patient, abiding person who gives and gives and never gets. A servant in this context is a contributor. Someone who invests themselves in the goals and objectives of the group, shares their motivation with others, and is a source of stability within a group.

The members of a group reach points in their projects where the need for leadership becomes obvious. This often happens when consensus cannot be reached, the scope of the project broadens, or additional departmental cooperation is required. The group looks within itself for a leader. This is a natural process within the framework of the group dynamic. They look for someone in whom they have trust and confidence. Someone who is equally invested in the outcome of the project and the groups objectives.

The person they choose may not be an obvious choice. Perhaps it isn't the person who makes the most noise or dominates group meetings. It may not even be the person who is the first in and last out at work every day. Who it will be is someone who the group determines feels with them and has something invested in their cause. Thus, the servant becomes a leader.

This leader can offer direction and guidance that is accepted without fear of hidden agendas or alternative motives. Because their roots are in the group and they have served the group, their motives and methods are rarely questioned. The group goals are furthered by mutual understanding and commitment to a successful outcome.

As I said, don't get the idea that a servant leader is some sort of selfless saint. They have much at stake in the success of their given group and are willing to both serve and lead. Often, there are rewards for assuming a leadership role and servant leaders are no different than other team members in welcoming these rewards. The difference is that they are willing to serve an informal internship to achieve these perks. Frequently the services of the servant leader are legitimized by promotion or some degree of elevation of status. But persons who achieve these promotions often do not have to deal with the infighting and jealously or co-workers because of how they achieved their status. They enjoy an acceptance that outsiders often don't get.

Look at your teams and just how they achieve results. Look for those "servant leaders" and recognize the valuable contributions they make. You can enrich the entire concept of team management by searching out these vital contributors who embody the truest definition of "team" and placing your trust in them just as their followers have done.

### *SITUATIONAL LEADERSHIP*

Different situations need to be dealt in a different ways; different people should also be dealt in diverse ways as well. Situational leadership theory states that a leader should not consider all the circumstances to be similar and apply the same methodology to deal with each one of them.

In fact different styles are recommended for to deal with new situations in order to get the desired outputs.

Hersey and Blanchard gave a model on situational leadership which is highly acclaimed. They believed that the leaders should be very flexible and should be able to adjust themselves to the new situations and new circumstances very quickly. Leadership style and Development level are the two concepts on which their model is based.

Situational leadership is flexible. It adapts to the existing work environment and the needs of the organization. Situational leadership is not based on a specific skill of the leader; instead, he or she modifies the style of management to suit the requirements of the organization.

One of the keys to situational leadership is adaptability. Leaders must be able to move from one leadership style to another to meet the changing needs of an organization and its employees. These leaders must have the insight to understand when to change their management style and what leadership strategy fits each new paradigm.

There are two mainstream models of situational leadership, one described by Daniel Goleman and another by Ken Blanchard and Paul Hershey.

Advantages and disadvantages of situational leadership

Situational leadership does not work well in all circumstances. Let's look at the advantages and disadvantages of the leadership style:

Situational leadership pros:

Easy to use: When a leader has the right style, he or she knows it

Simple: All the leader needs to do is evaluate the situation and apply the correct leadership style

Intuitive appeal: With the right type of leader, this style is comfortable

Leaders have permission to change management styles as they see fit

Situational leadership cons:

This North American style of leadership does not take into consideration priorities and communication styles of other cultures

It ignores the differences between female and male managers

Situational leaders can divert attention away from long-term strategies and politics

Benefits of situational leadership

"What is the best leadership style?" Hersey and Blanchard found it fruitless to provide one answer to this question. Everything depends on the specific situation, which is why they collaborated to develop the situational leadership model.

Situational leadership means "choosing the right leadership style for the right people," according to Blanchard and Hersey. It also depends on the competence and maturity of the followers. This is a time in history when leaders look less like bosses and more like partners.

Now that we've seen the three dominant leadership styles, which one are you? Remember that the mark of a good leader is the ability to use various styles depending on the situation - a bad leader sticks with the same style at all times. So what are some of the situations where each style is appropriate? If you have a new team, you may want to use the autocratic style as a means of assessing the group and its members. But what if you are placed in a position where most of the teams know their tasks well and would not react well to an autocratic stance? Use a participative style in this situation - allow the teams to have input in the decision making process. Remember that you can empower yourself as a leader as well as a team using this style. Finally, what if your team members know more about the situation than you do? Take a delegative approach and let the teams make their own decisions, all the while reminding them that you will be responsible for the outcomes.

When you're deciding what leadership style to take, there are a few things to consider. First of all, how much time do you have? If you're very limited in time, participative or autocratic may be the best style. Of course, this also depends on the team and its makeup - if you have an experienced team and limited time, there is no need to use an autocratic stance. Simply explain and emphasize that time is limited. You should also take into account who has the information related to the project or task at hand - if information is divided amongst you, the leader, and the team, you may want to take a participative stance. If your team has all of the information, take a delegative stance - let them use their information to come up with the best solutions. Also consider the type of task you're looking at - how complicated is it? Compare this with the skill of the team and you should be able to choose an appropriate leadership style.

If your dominant style is more autocratic, you may want to examine what's keeping you from moving into a participative stance. If you are one of the other two types, you're probably getting a good response from your teams. Just remember to alter your leadership style based on situations - and don't stick to one style regardless. When you begin to move around the different styles, you'll find that your teams will respond.

### *Do not go yet; One last thing to do*

If you enjoyed this book or found it useful I'd be very grateful if you'd post a short review on **Amazon**. Your support really does make a difference and I read all the reviews personally so I can get your feedback and make this book even better.

### *Thanks again for your support!*